CHAPTER 1

Eric Wizzard, the wizard's boy, was sitting on his front doorstep. He had his jacket in his hand and he was waiting for his mum.

MMMM! MMMUGH! MRRM!

He heard a strange noise above him.

The front door had just been painted
and the brass door-knocker was covered
in tape to stop the paint getting on it.

Eric stood up
and ripped off
a piece of tape...

...and another...

...and another...

He removed the last bit.

But the magical door-knocker always found something to moan about.

Eric stuck a bit of tape back over the door-knocker's mouth.

Just then the door opened.

Eric's dad came out.

Eric's mum was an airline pilot so she
was always flying round the world.
Sometimes she was late in getting home.

8

At that moment, Eric's dad saw the bit
of tape over the door-knocker's mouth.

He could have removed it by hand, but
being a wizard, he preferred magic. He
cast a spell.

Take off tape!

However, Eric's dad wasn't a very good wizard and his spells had the habit of going wrong.

The *'Take off tape!'* spell became *'Make odd shape!'* by mistake.

'I'm afraid we'll have to do the trip on our own,' said Dad.

So Eric and his dad and their dog
Theodore got into the car and headed
for the seaside.

CHAPTER 2

After driving for an hour they caught
sight of the sea.
'What would you like to do first?'
asked Eric's dad. 'Go to the beach or the
fairground?'
'The Mighty Monster Fairground!'
said Eric.

By the time they reached
the fairground,
Eric had counted his
money and knew
exactly what he
wanted to do.

This way!

They went on an aeroplane ride.

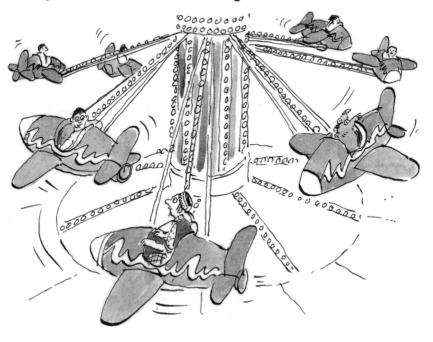

They ate ice-cream.

They went on the big dipper.

WHOOOSH!

They tried to knock down cans...

...and shook hands
with some of the
fairground staff
dressed in monster
costumes.

CHAPTER 3

Then the moment which Eric had been waiting for all morning arrived – a ride on the Grisly Ghost Train.

Eric's dad paid
for the ride and
they all got
into a car.

With a loud wail...

WVAAAAAAAAÀ!

...the doors opened and the car
moved into the darkness.

Eric felt something  **BRUSH** against his face.

Then a skull with green eyes and glowing teeth smiled a horrible smile.

The car swung out into the daylight
again and headed for Dracula's tower.

As they went in through a door,
Dracula began to sit up in his coffin...

...then the car stopped and everything
went quiet.

A voice called out...

Eric felt really annoyed as he had been so looking forward to this ride.

Eric realised he had broken his one golden
rule – if your dad's a hopeless wizard,
never ask him to fix anything by magic.

But it was too late, his dad was about
to cast a spell.

Bring back flow of power!

As usual, it went wrong and the spell became *'Drac spring out of the tower!'* which meant that Dracula...

...hopped out of the tower...

...and disappeared into the crowds.

Eric flew
into a panic.

His dad
thought hard.

Then he cast another spell.

But the spell came out as
'Monsters join Drac for walks!'

Now all the other monsters in the Grisly Ghost Ride were walking out.

CHAPTER 4

Eric and his dad climbed out of the
window.

They hurried through the fairground
and soon they caught sight of the
gorilla.

...to show it was really one of the fairground staff in a gorilla suit.

Now Eric and his dad didn't know which were the real monsters and which were people in monster suits.

There seemed to be monsters everywhere...

...and although Eric's dad had promised not to cast another spell, he had to try just one more.

But the spell came out as *'Give Wizzards monster faces!'*

Just then they heard the noise of
a siren.

A police car drew up at the fairground
and three policemen got out in a
hurry.

Eric's day at the fairground had turned
out to be a very strange one and it was
about to get even stranger.

CHAPTER 5

As they sat in the car wondering what to do next, something caught Eric's eye.

Hey, Dad!

Some monsters were running towards them.

In a moment, they had opened the car doors and jumped in.

The monsters pulled off their faces.

So Eric's dad drove the robbers to the airfield as quickly as he could.

They pulled up at the edge of the runway just as a plane landed.

There's Mick! Dead on time!

The robbers jumped out of the car
and Eric and his dad were told to
get out too.

They ran across
the runway...

...and piled into the plane. The pilot was wearing a mask, too.

The plane moved back down the runway...

...and took off.

CHAPTER 6

Just as the plane rose up, another passenger appeared from nowhere...

...and terrified the robbers.

The pilot turned the plane round and landed again.

As the wheels touched the ground, Dad's spells wore off.

Then the pilot took off the mask.

The plane was soon surrounded
by police cars and the robbers
were led away.

As they walked to the car, Eric's mum explained what had happened.

As I was late, I was able to borrow a plane from a pilot friend...

...so I could fly down here and join you.

I heard on the radio that there had been a raid.

I also heard the robbers talking on *their* radio. When these monsters jumped out of your car and ran towards my plane, I knew they had made a mistake.

I contacted the police...

...and pulled on this mask.

Back at home, the door-knocker was in a really bad mood.